Money Laundering:
A Banker's Guide to Avoiding Problems

Office of the Comptroller of the Currency

Washington, DC

December 2002

This booklet updates and expands upon the Office of the Comptroller of the Currency's (OCC's) prior publication, *Money Laundering: A Banker's Guide to Avoiding Problems* (second edition June 1993). This revision was prompted by the growing sophistication of money launderers, a growing international response to money laundering, changes to anti-money laundering laws, and recent anti-terrorist financing legislation.

This booklet presents basic background information on U.S. money-laundering laws and international anti-money laundering efforts. It also discusses actions bankers can take to better identify and manage risks associated with money laundering and terrorist financing. It is intended to provide a high-level discussion of concepts and issues. More detail on the subjects discussed may be obtained by using the listing of materials and organizations in the "Where to Get More Information" section.

Introduction

Over the past several years the banking industry, financial institutions, and the financial services industry have made significant strides in money laundering detection and prevention. However, they continue to be vulnerable to misuse by criminal elements for laundering illegally obtained profits and funds intended to finance terrorist activities.

Money-laundering methods have become more creative since the 1989 and 1993 versions of this booklet were published. This is due to the expansion of products and services offered, more complicated financial relationships, advances in technology, and the increased velocity of money flows worldwide. Terrorist financing, although only one aspect of money laundering, has become a critical concern following the events of September 11, 2001. The Office of the Comptroller of the Currency requires regulated institutions to develop and implement effective anti-money laundering programs that encompass terrorist financing. This has included record searches against U.S. government lists of suspected terrorists and terrorist organizations. The USA PATRIOT Act[1] contains provisions to combat international terrorism and block terrorist access to the U.S. financial system. Several international organizations have also issued measures to curb money laundering and terrorist financing.

---

[1] USA PATRIOT Act is the short name for H.R. 3162, entitled "The Uniting and Strengthening America by Providing Appropriate Tools Required to Intercept and Obstruct Terrorism." Title III of the Act is the International Money Laundering Abatement and Anti Terrorist Financing Act of 2001.

Background

Money laundering is the criminal practice of filtering ill-gotten gains or "dirty" money through a series of transactions, so that the funds are "cleaned" to look like proceeds from legal activities. Money laundering is driven by criminal activities and conceals the true source, ownership, or use of funds. The International Monetary Fund has stated that the aggregate size of money laundering in the world could be somewhere between 2 and 5 percent of the world's gross domestic product.

Money laundering is a diverse and often complex process that need not involve cash transactions. Money laundering basically involves three independent steps that can occur simultaneously:

- Placement - placing, through deposits or other means, unlawful proceeds into the financial system.

- Layering - separating proceeds of criminal activity from their origin through the use of layers of complex financial transactions.

- Integration - using additional transactions to create the appearance of legality through the purchase of assets.

An effective anti-money laundering program will help minimize exposure to transaction, compliance, and reputation risks. Such a program should include account opening controls and the monitoring and reporting of suspicious activity. Identifying possible terrorist financing may be a more difficult endeavor, since transactions may originate from legitimate sources and involve relatively small amounts of money.

Anti-Money Laundering and Anti-Terrorist Financing Legislation

Bank Secrecy Act and Related Anti-Money Laundering Laws

The U.S. has imposed many legislative and regulatory standards to help deter money laundering. The most significant of these are: the Bank Secrecy Act (Currency and Foreign Transactions Reporting Act of 1970); the Money Laundering Control Act of 1986; the Anti-Drug Abuse Act of 1988; Section 2532 of the Crime Control Act of 1990; Section 206 of the Federal Deposit Insurance Corporation Improvement Act of 1991; the Annunzio-Wylie Anti-Money Laundering Act (Title XV of the Housing and Community Development Act of 1992); the Money Laundering Suppression Act of 1994 (Title IV of the Riegle-Neal Community Development and Regulatory Improvement Act of 1994); the Money Laundering and Financial Crimes Strategy Act of 1998; and the USA PATRIOT Act (Title III, International Money Laundering Abatement and Anti-Terrorist Financing Act of 2001). Following are descriptions of these legislative measures.

The **Bank Secrecy Act (BSA)** was designed to fight drug trafficking, money laundering, and other crimes. Congress enacted the BSA to help prevent banks and other financial service providers from being used as intermediaries for, or being used to hide the transfer or deposit of money derived from, criminal activity. Among other items, the BSA created an investigative "paper trail" by establishing regulatory reporting standards and requirements (e.g., the Currency Transaction Report), and, through a later amendment, established recordkeeping requirements for wire transfers. The OCC monitors national bank compliance with the BSA and the implementing regulations 31 CFR 103.

The **Money Laundering Control Act of 1986** amended the BSA to enhance its effectiveness and to strengthen the government's ability to fight money laundering by making it a federal crime and by making structuring transactions to avoid BSA reporting requirements a criminal offense.

The **Anti-Drug Abuse Act of 1988** reinforced and supplemented anti-money laundering efforts by increasing the levels of penalties and sanctions for money laundering crimes and by requiring strict identification and documentation of cash purchases of certain monetary instruments.

Section 2532 of the Crime Control Act of 1990 enhanced the federal banking agencies enforcement position by giving it powers to work with foreign banking authorities on investigations, examinations, or enforcement actions dealing with possible bank or currency transaction-related violations.

Section 206 of The Federal Deposit Insurance Corporation Improvement Act (FDICIA) of 1991 allowed the OCC and other bank supervisory authorities some latitude in disclosing to foreign bank regulatory or supervisory authorities information obtained during its supervisory role. Such disclosure must be appropriate, not prejudice the interests of the U.S., and must be subject to appropriate measures of confidentiality.

The **Annunzio-Wylie Anti-Money Laundering Act of 1992** increased penalties for depository institutions found guilty of money laundering. The act added several significant provisions to the BSA, including the reporting of suspicious transactions. The act also made the operation of an illegal money transmitting business a crime, and required that banking regulatory agencies formally consider revoking the charter of any depository institution convicted of money laundering.

The **Money Laundering Suppression Act of 1994** required regulators to develop enhanced examination procedures and to increase examiner training to improve the identification of money laundering schemes in financial institutions.

The **Money Laundering and Financial Crimes Strategy Act of 1998** required the Secretary of the Treasury, in consultation with the Attorney General and other relevant agencies, including state and local agencies, to coordinate and implement a national strategy to address money laundering.

The **USA PATRIOT Act** evolved as a response by the U.S. government to combat international terrorism. The act contained strong measures to prevent, detect, and prosecute terrorism and international money laundering. Signed into law on October 26, 2001, the act establishes new rules and responsibilities affecting U.S. banking organizations, other financial institutions, and non-financial commercial businesses. The act:

- Provides the Secretary of the Treasury with the authority to impose special measures on jurisdictions, institutions, or transactions that are of "primary money-laundering concern."

- Requires financial institutions to increase their due diligence standards when dealing with foreign private banking and correspondent accounts.

- Prohibits correspondent accounts with foreign "shell" banks.

- Expands the ability of the public and private sectors to share information related to terrorism and money laundering investigations.

- Facilitates records access and requires banks to respond to regulatory requests for information within 120 hours.

- Establishes minimum standards for customer identification at account opening and requires checks against government-provided lists of known or suspected terrorists.

- Requires regulatory agencies to evaluate an institution's anti-money laundering record when considering bank mergers, acquisitions, and other applications for business combinations.

- Extends an anti-money laundering program requirement to all financial institutions.

- Increases the civil and criminal penalties for money laundering.

International Anti-Money Laundering and Anti-Terrorist Financing Initiatives

The international community has long recognized that the problems of money laundering and terrorism require a coordinated approach. For many years, a number of international organizations have developed standards for combating money laundering, terrorism, and terrorist financing. These standards contain common themes of promoting actions to deny criminals, terrorists, and those who assist them access to their funds and the world's financial services industries. Many international agreements and resolutions outline similar standards or build upon each other.

The Financial Action Task Force on Money Laundering (FATF) is an important inter-governmental body that develops and promotes policies to combat money laundering. It focuses on:

- Spreading the anti-money laundering message to all continents and regions of the globe.

- Monitoring the implementation of its Forty Recommendations.

- Reviewing and publishing money laundering trends and countermeasures ("typologies exercise").

FATF fosters the creation of a worldwide anti-money laundering network based on the development of regional anti-money laundering bodies, close co-operation with relevant international organizations, and expansion of its membership. FATF's Forty Recommendations set a framework for anti-money laundering efforts and are designed for universal application. Initially developed in 1990, they were revised in 1996 to take into account changes in money laundering trends and to anticipate potential threats. Currently, the FATF is working on another update to their Forty Recommendations.

An Extraordinary Plenary held in Washington, D.C., in October 2001 formally broadened FATF's mission beyond anti-money laundering to include anti-terrorist financing. FATF developed an action plan to address terrorist financing and issued new international standards called the Special Recommendations on Terrorist Financing. In implementing the new action plan, FATF will intensify its cooperation with the FATF-style regional bodies and international organizations that support and contribute to the international effort against money laundering and terrorist financing. FATF also agreed to consider the Special Recommendations as it revises its Forty Recommendations on Money Laundering and to intensify its work on corporate vehicles, correspondent banking, identification of beneficial owners of accounts, and regulation of nonbank financial institutions.

FATF has formulated additional guidance on the techniques and mechanisms used in the financing of terrorism. FATF's "Report on Money Laundering Typologies Report 2001-2002" and "Guidance for Financial Institutions in Detecting Terrorist Financing" were issued in February 2002 and April 2002, respectively.

What Bankers Can Do To Help

This section highlights fundamental controls that are important for effective anti-money laundering systems and legal compliance. These controls include effective BSA compliance and customer due diligence programs, compliance with Office of Foreign Assets Control (OFAC) guidelines, suspicious activity monitoring and reporting systems, and risk-based anti-money laundering programs.

Establish Effective BSA Compliance Programs

Banks must have a BSA compliance program. National banks, as outlined in 12 CFR 21.21, must develop, administer, and maintain a program that ensures and monitors compliance with the BSA, including record keeping and reporting requirements. A bank's compliance program must be written, approved by the board of directors, and noted as such in the board meeting minutes. The program must also contain:

- A system of internal controls to ensure ongoing BSA compliance.
- Daily coordination and monitoring of compliance by a designated person.
- Training for appropriate personnel.
- Independent testing of compliance (by internal auditors or an outside party).

Establish Effective Customer Due Diligence Systems and Monitoring Programs

Comprehensive customer due diligence programs are banks' most effective weapons against being used unwittingly to launder money or to support terrorist financing. Knowing customers, including depositors and other users of bank services, requiring appropriate identification, and being alert to unusual or suspicious transactions can help deter and detect money laundering and terrorist financing schemes. Effective due diligence systems are also fundamental to help ensure compliance with suspicious activity reporting regulations.

These regulations require banks to report transactions that have no apparent lawful purpose or are not the sort in which the particular customer would be expected to engage.

The first and most essential step in effective customer due diligence is verifying the identity of the customer. Present guidelines for the opening of personal accounts include: obtain satisfactory customer identification; consider the proximity of the customer's residence or place of business; call-verify the customer's residence or place of employment; consider the source of funds used to open the account; and check prior banking references for larger accounts. Additional steps may include third-party references, verification services, and the use of Internet search techniques. In addition to verifying the legal status of businesses opening accounts, bankers should determine the source of funds and the beneficial owners of all accounts. The existence of most businesses can be verified through an information-reporting agency, banking references, or by visiting the customer's business.

The USA PATRIOT Act addresses several aspects of due diligence at account opening.

- Verification of Identification - Prescribes minimum standards that financial institutions must follow to verify the identity of both foreign and domestic customers at account opening. Financial institutions must consult U.S. government-provided lists of known or suspected terrorists or terrorist organizations and keep records of the information used to verify each customer's identity.

- Special Due Diligence for Correspondent and Private Banking Accounts - Sets forth general due diligence standards and provides additional standards for certain correspondent accounts and minimum standards for private banking accounts of non-U.S. persons.

Once the bank has established a customer relationship, it should be alert for unusual transactions. Although attempts to launder money through a financial institution can emanate from many different sources, certain products and services, types of entities, and geographic locations are more vulnerable to money laundering and/or terrorist financing. Accordingly, greater due diligence standards should occur for higher risk relationships, both at the account opening and ongoing account activity stages.

Screen Against OFAC and Other Government Lists

OFAC administers and enforces economic and trade sanctions against targeted foreign countries, terrorism-sponsoring organizations, and international narcotics traffickers based on U.S. foreign policy and national security goals. OFAC acts under presidential wartime and national emergency powers and the authority granted by specific legislation to impose controls on transactions and to freeze foreign assets under U.S. jurisdiction. Many of the sanctions are based on United Nations and other international mandates, are multilateral in scope, and involve close cooperation with allied countries. OFAC has promulgated regulations to help administer its sanctions program. All U.S. persons and entities, including banks, federal branches and agencies, international banking facilities, and overseas branches, offices and subsidiaries of U.S. banks must comply with the laws and OFAC-issued regulations. In general, these regulations:

- Require blocking of accounts and other assets of specified countries, entities, and persons.

- Prohibit unlicensed trade and financial transactions with specified countries, entities, and persons.

U.S. law requires that assets and accounts be blocked when such property is located in the United States, is held by U.S. persons or entities, or comes into the possession or control of U.S. persons or entities. The definition of assets and property is broad and includes anything of direct, indirect, present, future, and contingent value (including all types of bank transactions).

Banks should establish and maintain effective OFAC compliance programs. This program should include written policies and procedures for checking transactions for possible OFAC violations, designating a person responsible for day-to-day compliance, establishing and maintaining strong lines of communication between departments of the bank, employee training, and an annual in-depth audit of OFAC compliance. The compliance program should also include procedures for maintaining current lists of blocked countries, entities, and persons and for disseminating such information throughout the bank's domestic operations and its offshore branches and offices. All new accounts, including deposit, loan, trust, or other relationships must be compared with the OFAC lists when accounts are opened. Established accounts should be compared regularly with the current and updated OFAC lists. Wire transfers, letters of credit, and non-customer transactions, such as funds transfers, should be compared with the OFAC lists before being conducted.

Federal law enforcement may request information about suspected terrorists and money launderers relevant to investigations. Bankers must review their records for accounts and transactions and notify the Financial Crimes Enforcement Network (FinCEN) of any "matches" in accordance with the instructions provided.

Establish an Effective Suspicious Activity Monitoring and Reporting Process

An effective BSA compliance program includes controls and measures to identify and report suspicious transactions promptly. Financial institutions must employ appropriate customer due diligence to effectively evaluate transactions and conclude whether to file a suspicious activity report (SAR).

Banks must file SARs within prescribed timeframes. SARs must be filed following the discovery of transactions aggregating $5,000 or more that involve potential money laundering or violations of the BSA if the bank knows, suspects, or has reason to suspect that the transaction:

- Involves funds from illegal activities or is conducted to hide illicit funds or assets in a plan to violate or evade any law or regulation or to avoid transaction reporting requirements under federal law.

What Bankers Can Do

- Is designed to evade any of the BSA regulations.

- Has no business or apparent lawful purpose or is not the sort in which the customer would normally be expected to engage, and the bank knows of no reasonable explanation for the transaction after examining available facts, including the background and transaction purpose.

The bank's board of directors must be notified of SAR filings, and such filings and information contained therein must remain confidential, unless properly requested by law enforcement. Financial institutions are protected from liability to customers for disclosures of possible violations of law under safe harbor provisions. Additionally, the safe harbor covers all reports (including supporting SAR documentation) of suspected or known criminal violations and suspicious activities to law enforcement and the financial institution's supervisory authority.

There are more than 200 predicate crimes for money laundering. These include funds that support terrorist activity, profits from illegal drug sales, and structuring of transactions to avoid record keeping and reporting requirements. A bank does not have to conduct an investigation to determine if funds were derived illegally. Instead, banks must report suspicious activity. Law enforcement will determine if a predicate crime associated with the funds has been violated.

Develop Risk-Based Anti-Money Laundering Programs

Bank anti-money laundering programs should be structured to address the controls needed based on the risks posed by the products and services offered, customers served, and geographies. The following are examples of high-risk products and services, customers, and geographic locations of which banks should be aware when developing a risk-based anti-money laundering program.

High-Risk Products and Services

Wire Transfer/International Correspondent Banking - Money launderers have become more creative in their use of wire transfer systems, particularly relating to correspondent bank accounts. Correspondent accounts are accounts banks maintain with each other to facilitate transactions for themselves and their customers. Although these accounts were developed and are used primarily for legitimate purposes, international correspondent bank accounts may pose increased risk of illicit activities. The Minority Staff of the U.S. Senate Permanent Subcommittee on Investigations issued a report on February 5, 2001, entitled "Correspondent Banking and Money Laundering." The report summarizes a year-long investigation into correspondent banking and its use as a tool for laundering money. The investigation found that U.S. banks through international correspondent accounts could become conduits for dirty money flowing into the American financial system.

Bankers must exercise due diligence in determining risks associated with each of their foreign correspondent accounts. Factors to consider include account purpose, location of the foreign bank, nature of the banking license, the correspondent's money laundering detection and prevention controls, and the extent of bank regulation and supervision in the foreign country. The USA PATRIOT Act also requires the maintenance of certain records for foreign correspondent accounts, mandates enhanced due diligence for select accounts, and precludes maintaining correspondent accounts for "shell" banks.

Private Banking Relationships - Private banking has many definitions, but generally is considered the personal or discreet offering of a wide variety of financial services and products to the affluent market. These operations typically offer all-inclusive personalized services. Individuals, commercial businesses, law firms, investment advisors, trusts, and personal investment companies may open private banking accounts. Due diligence for private banking clients usually includes a more extensive process than for retail customers, including confirming references and/or conducting background checks. It is critical to understand a client's source of wealth, needs, and expected transactions. The private banking client's expected level and type of transactions should be documented. Private banking relationships can be complex and systems to monitor and report suspicious activity should be designed to reasonably evaluate the client's total activities.

Senior foreign public officials are often private banking clients. In January 2001, "Guidance on Enhanced Scrutiny for Transactions that May Involve the Proceeds of Foreign Official Corruption" was issued by the Department of Treasury, the Office of the Comptroller of the Currency, the Office of Thrift Supervision, the Board of Governors of the Federal Reserve System, the Federal Deposit Insurance Corporation, and the Department of State. The guidance contains suggested procedures for account opening and monitoring for persons known to be senior foreign political figures, their immediate family members and their close associates. It also contains a list of questionable or suspicious activities that may warrant enhanced scrutiny of transactions involving such persons. In addition, the USA PATRIOT Act requires enhanced due diligence and scrutiny for private banking accounts requested or maintained by senior foreign political figures, their immediate family members, and their close associates. U.S. financial institutions should apply these principles and requirements to private banking activities and accounts.

Electronic Banking - Electronic banking is a broad term encompassing delivery of information, products, and services by electronic means (such as telephone lines, personal computers, automated teller machines, and automated clearing houses). This product offering continues to grow at a rapid pace. Although the extent of services varies, typical Internet bank services include credit cards, loans, deposits, wire transfers, and bill-paying services. Electronic banking is vulnerable to money laundering and terrorist financing because of its user anonymity, rapid transaction speed, and its wide geographic availability.

High-Risk Customers

Certain kinds of businesses may require enhanced customer due diligence at account opening and ongoing transaction review. Banks should conduct a risk assessment and ensure that controls are proportionate to the customer's risk level. The following should be considered when doing business with high-risk customers: their anti-money laundering systems; potential for being abused by money launderers; their level of risk; and the bank's ability to control that risk. Entities that traditionally have been identified as high-risk include:

- Nonbank Financial Institutions (NBFI), including Money Service Businesses - Typical examples include security brokers and dealers, check-cashing services, currency dealers and exchangers, and issuers, sellers, or redeemers of traveler's checks, money orders, or stored value cards. Card clubs, gambling casinos, and money transmitters are also NBFIs.

- Non-governmental organizations (e.g. charitable organizations).

- Offshore corporations, bearer share corporations, and banks located in tax and/or secrecy havens and jurisdictions designated as non-cooperative in the fight against money laundering.

- Cash-intensive businesses (convenience stores, parking garages, restaurants, retail stores).

High-Risk Geographic Locations

Identifying high-risk geographic locations is essential to a bank's anti-money laundering program. U.S. banks should understand and evaluate the specific risks associated with doing business in, opening accounts for customers from, or facilitating transactions involving high-risk geographic locations. Information regarding possible high-risk geographic locations is available from several sources including:

- Jurisdictions identified by intergovernmental organizations (e.g., FATF) as non-cooperative in the fight against money laundering. Such locations have become widely known as non-cooperative countries and territories (NCCT).

- Countries/jurisdictions identified by the U.S. Department of State's annual International Narcotics Control Strategy Report (INCSR) as "primary concern."

- Geographies identified by OFAC.

- Jurisdictions designated by the Secretary of the Treasury as being of primary money laundering concern as authorized by the USA PATRIOT Act.

- Jurisdictions identified by bank management.

Identifying customers and transactions from high-risk geographic locations is crucial in controlling money laundering and terrorist financing risk. By obtaining such information, bankers can develop or modify policies, procedures, and controls addressing the risks associated with those locations.

What Bankers Should Look For

The following are examples of potentially suspicious activities or "red flags" for both money laundering and terrorist financing. These lists are not all-inclusive, but may help bankers recognize possible money laundering and terrorist financing schemes. Banks should be focused primarily on reporting suspicious transactions, not on determining that the transactions are in fact linked to money laundering or terrorist financing.

The examples mentioned may warrant attention, but simply because a transaction appears on the list does not mean it involves suspicious activity. Closer scrutiny will help determine whether the transactions or activities reflect suspicious activities rather than legitimate business activities and whether a SAR should be filed.

Money Laundering Red Flags

Customers Who Provide Insufficient or Suspicious Information

- A customer uses unusual or suspicious identification documents that cannot be readily verified.

- A business is reluctant, when establishing a new account, to provide complete information about the nature and purpose of its business, anticipated account activity, prior banking relationships, names of its officers and directors, or information on its business location.

- A customer's home/business telephone is disconnected.

- The customer's background differs from that which would be expected based on his or her business activities.

- A customer makes frequent or large transactions and has no record of past or present employment experience.

Efforts to Avoid Reporting or Record Keeping Requirement

- A customer or group tries to persuade a bank employee to not file required reports or to not maintain required records.

- A customer is reluctant to provide information needed to file a mandatory report, to have the report filed, or to proceed with a transaction after being informed that the report must be filed.

- A customer is reluctant to furnish identification when purchasing negotiable instruments in recordable amounts.

- A business or new customer asks to be exempted from reporting or record-keeping requirements.

- A customer uses the automated teller machine to make several bank deposits below a specified threshold.

Certain Funds Transfer Activities

- Wire transfer activity to/from a financial secrecy haven, or high-risk geographic location without an apparent business reason, or when it is inconsistent with the customer's business or history.

- Many small, incoming wire transfers of funds received, or deposits made using checks and money orders. Almost immediately, all or most are wired to another city or country in a manner inconsistent with the customer's business or history.

- Large incoming wire transfers on behalf of a foreign client with little or no explicit reason.

- Wire activity that is unexplained, repetitive, or shows unusual patterns.

- Payments or receipts with no apparent links to legitimate contracts, goods, or services.

Activity Inconsistent with the Customer's Business

- The currency transaction patterns of a business show a sudden change inconsistent with normal activities.

- A large volume of cashier's checks, money orders, and/or wire transfers deposited into, or purchased through, an account when the nature of the account holder's business would not appear to justify such activity.

- A retail business has dramatically different patterns of cash deposits from similar businesses in the same general location.

- Unusual transfer of funds among related accounts, or accounts that involve the same or related principals.

- The owner of both a retail business and a check-cashing service does not ask for cash when depositing checks, possibly indicating the availability of another source of cash.

Other Suspicious Customer Activity

- Frequent exchanges of small dollar denominations for large dollar denominations.

- Frequent deposits of currency wrapped in currency straps or currency wrapped in rubber bands that are disorganized and do not balance when counted.

- A customer who purchases a number of cashier's checks, money orders, or traveler's checks for large amounts under a specified threshold.

- Money orders deposited by mail, which are numbered sequentially or have unusual symbols or stamps on them.

- Suspicious movements of funds from one bank into another, then back into the first bank: 1) purchasing cashier's checks from bank A; 2) opening up a checking account at bank B; 3) depositing the cashier's checks into a checking account at bank B; and, 4) wire transferring the funds from the checking account at bank B into an account at bank A.

Changes in Bank-to-Bank Transactions

- A rapid increase in the size and frequency of cash deposits with no corresponding increase in non-cash deposits.

- Inability to track the true account holder of correspondent or concentration account transactions.

- Significant turnover in large denomination bills that would appear uncharacteristic given the bank's location.

- Significant changes in currency shipment patterns between correspondent banks.

Bank Employees

- Lavish lifestyle that cannot be supported by an employee's salary.

- Failure to conform with recognized systems and controls, particularly in private banking.

- Reluctance to take a vacation.

Terrorist Financing Red Flags

Identifying suspicious transactions that may be indicative of terrorist financing is a relatively new and difficult endeavor. Traditionally, anti-money laundering programs have focused on large, suspicious cash and non-cash transactions, both domestic and international. Terrorist financing may also involve smaller dollar amounts entering the country, and the funds may often be used in typical retail consumer activity. The risk of terrorist financing may exist in a variety of bank products and services. The risk of this activity may be higher in larger institutions and domestic branches of foreign banks, because of the international nature of their businesses, and size and breadth of their international branch and affiliate networks.

Banks should use recently published terrorist financing guidance when developing risk-based anti-money laundering programs. Recent publications that shed light on terrorist financing include the FATF Report on Money Laundering Typologies,[2] FATF Guidance for Financial Institutions in Detecting Terrorist Financing Activities, the FinCEN SAR Bulletin Issue 4, "Aspects of Financial Transactions Indicative of Terrorist Funding" published January 2002, and the 2002 National Money Laundering Strategy.

The FATF Guidance discusses similar methods of laundering funds by terrorist organizations and organized crime, though their motives may differ. The report also notes that terrorist groups have increasingly resorting to criminal activity to raise funds. With the exception of three activities, there is little difference in the funding sources currently used by terrorists and organized crime groups. The three funding activities distinct to terrorism include:

- Direct sponsorship by certain states.

- Contributions and donations.

- Sale of publications (legal and illegal).

FinCEN's SAR Bulletin Issue 4 contains a number of "red flags." Many are similar to the money laundering red flags listed previously; however, some are indicative of terrorist financing. They are:

- Funds generated by a business owned by nationals of countries associated with terrorist activity.

- Charity/relief organization-linked transactions.

- Currency exchange buying/selling foreign currencies from various countries in the Middle East.

---

[2] Financial Action Task Force on Money Laundering; Report on Money Laundering Typologies 2001 2002; pages 2 7. Financial Action Task Force on Money Laundering; Report on Money Laundering Typologies 2000 2001; pages 19 21.

- Business account activity conducted by nationals of foreign countries associated with terrorist activity with no obvious connection to the business.

On February 12, 2002, the U.S. House Financial Services Subcommittee on Oversight and Investigations heard testimony regarding terrorist financing and the implementation of the USA PATRIOT Act. The testimony discusses what the Federal Bureau of Investigation (FBI) has learned since the September 11, 2001, terrorist attacks about the patterns of financing associated with terrorist networks. The FBI also described the extent to which U.S. anti-money laundering statutes provide the necessary tools to detect and disrupt these patterns of financing. An interagency Financial Review Group devoted significant resources to identifying and following the money trail.

Reports That Can Help Bankers Identify Suspicious Transactions

A number of readily available reports, in addition to the OFAC List, the NCCT List, and other government lists, can be generated by banks to assist them in the fight against money laundering. Following are some internal reports routinely available through bank service providers.

Cash Transaction Reports - Most bank information service providers offer reports that identify cash activity and/or cash activity greater than $10,000. These reports assist bankers with filing currency transaction reports (CTRs) and in identifying suspicious cash activity. Some larger banks have software systems to assist them in completing CTRs accurately, especially when they have multiple locations. Most vendor software systems include standard suspicious cash activity reports that typically filter cash activity in three forms: 1) cash activity including multiple transactions greater than $10,000; 2) cash activity (single and multiple transactions) just below the $10,000 reporting threshold (e.g., between $8,000 - $10,000); and, 3) cash transactions involving multiple lower-dollar transactions (e.g., $3,000) which over a period of time (e.g., 15 days) aggregate to a substantial sum of money. Such filtering reports, when implemented either through the purchase of a vender software system or through requests from the information service provider, will enhance significantly a bank's ability to identify and evaluate unusual cash transactions.

Wire Transfer Records / Logs - The BSA requires wire transfer records. Periodic review of this information can assist banks in identifying patterns of unusual activity. A periodic review of the wire records/logs in banks with low wire transfer activity is usually sufficient to identify unusual activity. For banks with greater wire activity, use of spreadsheets or vendor software, is an efficient way to review wire activity for unusual patterns. Most vendor software systems include standard suspicious activity filter reports. These reports typically focus on identifying certain higher risk geographies and larger dollar wire transactions (persons and corporations). Each bank should establish its own filtering criteria for both personal and corporate wire volumes based on their customer base. Non-customer wire transactions and Pay Upon Proper Identification (PUPID) transactions should always be reviewed for unusual activity.

Monetary Instrument Records – Records on monetary instrument sales are required in certain circumstances by the BSA. Such records can assist bankers in identifying possible currency structuring[3] through the purchase of cashier's checks, money orders, or traveler's checks in amounts of $3,000 to $10,000. A periodic review of these records can also help identify frequent purchasers and remitters of monetary instruments and common payees.

Velocity of Funds Report - A velocity of funds report reflects the total debits and credits flowing through a particular account over a specific period (e.g., 30 days). This report can be used to identify customer accounts with substantial funds flow relative to other accounts. A review of this information can assist bankers to identify customers with a high velocity of funds flow and those with unusual activity.

---

[3] Currency structuring is defined as actions taken by a customer or individual(s) to avoid BSA reporting requirements (e.g. currency transaction reports). Structuring as defined by the Bank Secrecy Act is a criminal offense.

Schemes Involving Possible Money Laundering and Terrorist Financing

Below are a series of real cases selected from published reports. They are provided to reinforce the need for comprehensive, board-approved customer due diligence policies, a BSA compliance program, and sound suspicious activity monitoring systems. They also highlight the risks banks become subject to in the absence of a sound anti-money laundering program.

Russian Money Laundering Scandal

This scandal became public during the summer of 1999, with media reports of $7 billion in suspect funds moving from two Russian banks through a U.S. bank to thousands of bank accounts throughout the world. Pleadings from subsequent criminal cases indicate that, during a four-year period from 1995-1999, two Russian banks deposited more than $7 billion in correspondent bank accounts at a New York bank. After successfully gaining entry for these funds into the U.S. banking system, the Russian banks transferred amounts from their New York bank correspondent accounts to commercial accounts at the bank that had been opened for three shell corporations. These three corporations, in turn, transferred the funds to thousands of other bank accounts around the world, using electronic wire transfer software provided by the bank. In the aggregate, from February 1996 through August 1999, the three corporations completed more than 160,000 wire transfers.

In February 2000, guilty pleas were submitted by a bank employee and spouse and the three corporations for conspiracy to commit money laundering, operating an unlawful banking and money transmitting business in the United States, and aiding/ abetting Russian banks in conducting unlawful and unlicensed banking activities in the United States. The defendants admitted their money-laundering scheme was designed, in part, to help Russian individuals/businesses transfer funds in violation of Russian currency controls, custom duties, and taxes. The three corporations agreed to forfeit more than $6 million in their New York bank accounts. In August 2000, a federal court held that the United States had sufficient facts to establish probable cause to seize another $27 million from two New York correspondent accounts belonging to a Russian bank.

Operation Wire Cutter

The U.S. Customs Service, in conjunction with the Drug Enforcement Administration (DEA) and Colombian Departamento Administrativo de Seguridad, arrested 37 people in January 2002 as a result of a two-and-one-half-year undercover investigation of Colombian peso brokers and their money laundering organizations. These people are believed to have laundered money for several Colombian narcotics cartels. The peso brokers contacted undercover Customs agents and directed them to pick-up currency in New York, Miami, Chicago, Los Angeles, and San Juan, Puerto Rico, that had been generated from narcotics transactions. The brokers subsequently directed the undercover agents to wire these proceeds to specified accounts in U.S. financial institutions that were often in the name of Colombian companies or banks that had a correspondent account with a U.S. bank. Laundered monies were subsequently withdrawn from banks in Colombia in Colombian pesos. Investigators seized more than $8 million in cash, 400 kilos of cocaine, 100 kilos of marijuana, 6.5 kilos of heroin, nine firearms, and six vehicles.

Khalil Khurfan Organization

The DEA (New York Division Group) and the U.S. Attorney's Office in the Southern District of New York concluded a long-term investigation targeting the money laundering and narcotics activities of the Khalil Kharfan Organization operating in Colombia, Puerto Rico, Florida, and the New York Tri-State area. To date, the investigation has revealed that this organization laundered in excess of $100 million in narcotics proceeds. The organization was extremely sophisticated and used several types of communication devices to expedite the transfer of funds worldwide. The Colombian cell, which had staff stationed domestically in Puerto Rico, Florida, New York, and New Jersey, and international businesses and banks in

Panama, Israel, Switzerland, and Colombia, used "members" to open accounts in the names of fictitious businesses allowing monies to be deposited and then transferred. Approximately $1 million has been seized.

High-Risk Geographic Location

A pattern of cash deposits below the CTR reporting threshold generated a SAR filing by a U.S. institution. Deposits were made daily to the account of a foreign currency exchange totaling $341,421 for approximately a two-and-one-half-month period. During the same period, the business initiated 10 wire transfers totaling $2.7 million to a bank in the United Arab Emirates. When questioned, the business owner reportedly indicated he was in the business of buying/selling foreign currencies in Iran, the Persian Gulf States, and other countries in the Middle East, and his business never generated in excess of $10,000 a day. CTRs for three years reflected cash deposits totaling $137,470 and withdrawals totaling $29,387. The business owner and the cash-out transactions were conducted by nationals of countries associated with terrorist activity. Another U.S. depository institution filed a SAR on this person for an $80,000 cash deposit, which was deemed unusual for his profession. He also cashed two negotiable instruments at the same depository institution for $68,000 and $16,387 according to CTR filings.

Wire Remittance Company

Both a wire remittance company and a depository institution filed SARs outlining the movement of about $7 million in money orders through the U.S. account of a foreign business. The wire remittance company reported various persons purchasing money orders at the maximum face value of $500 to $1,000 and in sequential order. Purchases were made at multiple locations, primarily in the northeastern United States, and several purchases also were reported in the southeast United States. The money orders were made payable to various persons, negotiated through banks in Lebanon, and later cleared through three U.S. institutions. The foreign business endorsed the money orders. In some instances, the funds were then credited to accounts at other U.S. depository institutions or foreign institutions. SARs filed by the depository institution reported similar purchases of money orders in the northeastern United States negotiated at the foreign business. Various beneficiaries were identified, all with Middle Eastern names. They received amounts ranging from $5,000 to $11,000. The foreign business identified by the wire remittance company also was identified as a secondary beneficiary. The money orders cleared through a foreign bank's cash letter account at the U.S. depository institution.

Travel Agent

An IRS investigation in Virginia was initiated on the owner of a travel agency for currency structuring charges after analysis of SAR and CTR filings. The suspect operated, in addition to the travel agency, a money transmittal business that was wiring funds to his business interests in Lima, Peru, and Bogota, Colombia. An analysis of subsequent SARs and CTRs, coupled with various investigative techniques, including execution of several search warrants, led to the suspect entering a plea to one count of money laundering. The defendant admitted structuring transactions to avoid a CTR filing. The defendant structured deposits totaling between $2.5 to $5 million and used six business accounts at five financial institutions to facilitate his activities. The defendant consented to the administrative forfeiture of monies seized from his business accounts.

Suspicious Activity Report Leads to Embargo Investigation

An investigation of a possible violation of the International Emergency Economic Powers Act was initiated following a SAR filing by a bank in New York. The SAR stated that an unnamed bank vice president in charge of the funds transfer program manipulated four payments to the Sudan totaling $73,000 in violation of the embargo. The subject allegedly manipulated the bank's internal Office of Foreign Assets Control (OFAC) filtering system by either manually overriding its screening and blocking function or by omitting any reference to Sudan and reprocessing the wire transfers through the same filtering system. The case was turned over to OFAC.

Where To Get More Information

OFFICE OF THE COMPTROLLER OF THE CURRENCY

For information on money laundering and national banks, contact:

Compliance Division
(202) 874-4428

For OCC Publications and Ordering Information, contact:

Communications Division
Office of the Comptroller of the Currency
250 E Street, SW
Washington, DC 20219-0001
(202) 874-4700

http://www.occ.treas.gov/mail1.htm

For information on establishing a BSA Compliance Program, refer to OCC's Comptroller's Handbooks:

Bank Secrecy Act/Anti-Money Laundering

http://www.occ.treas.gov/handbook/bsa.pdf

DOMESTIC ANTI-MONEY LAUNDERING AND TERRORIST FINANCING RESOURCES

Bank Secrecy Act

http://cfr.law.cornell.edu/cfr/cfr.php?title=31&type=part&value=103

Financial Crimes Enforcement Network (FinCEN)
Office of Enforcement and Regulation
U.S. Department of the Treasury
270 Chain Bridge Road, Suite 200
Vienna, VA 22182
(800) 949-2732 *(Regulatory Help Line)*
(866) 556-3974 *(Hotline for Suspected Terrorist Related Activity)*

http://www.ustreas.gov/fincen/

FinCEN – Regulatory / BSA Forms and Filing Information
http://www.treas.gov/fincen/bsaf_main.html

FinCEN – Publications / Advisories, Bulletins, Rulings, Fact Sheets

http://www.treas.gov/fincen/pub main.html

FinCEN – Publications / External Documents

http://www.treas.gov/fincen/pub external reports.html

Office of Foreign Asset Control (OFAC)

U.S. Department of the Treasury
Treasury Annex
1500 Pennsylvania Avenue, NW
Washington, DC 20220
Compliance Hotline: (202) 622-2490
OFAC Fax-on-demand: (202) 622-2480

http://www.treas.gov/ofac

OFAC - Regulations for the Financial Community

http://www.ustreas.gov/offices/enforcement/ofac/regulations/
index.html

United States Department of State:

The "International Narcotics Control Strategy Report (INCSR)"
for 2001

http://www.state.gov/g/inl/rls/nrcrpt/2001/

OTHER FINANCIAL SERVICE RESOURCES

American Bankers Association

1120 Connecticut Avenue, NW
Washington, DC 20036
(800)-Bankers
http://www.aba.com/

Bankers Association Institute
One North Franklin•
Suite 1000•
Chicago, Illinois 60606-3421•
(800) 224-9889 •
http://www.bai.org/contact•

International Association of Insurance Supervisors
http://www.iaisweb.org

Guidance Papers: Anti-Money Laundering Guidance Notes for
Insurance Supervisors & Insurance Entities
http://www.iaisweb.org/content/02pas/02money.pdf

Securities Industry Association
http://www.sia.com/

**Frequently Asked Questions and Answers About Financial
Services Industry's Efforts To End Money Laundering**
http://www.sia.com/press/html/moneylaundering.html

U.S. General Accounting Office
441 G Street, NW
Washington, DC 20548
(202) 512-6000
http://www.gao.gov/index.html

INTERNATIONAL ORGANIZATIONS AND AGREEMENTS

Financial Action Task Force on Money Laundering (FATF)
http://www.fatf-gafi.org/

FATF – Forty Recommendations
http://www.fatf-gafi.org/40Recs en.htm

FATF – Special Recommendations on Terrorist Financing
http://www.fatf-gafi.org/SRecsTF en.htm

FATF – Guidance for Financial Institutions in Detecting Terrorist Financing
http://www.fatf-gafi.org/pdf/GuidFITF01 en.pdf

FATF – Non-Cooperative Countries and Territories (NCCT) Information
http://www.fatf-gafi.org/NCCT en.htm

Bank for International Settlements
http://www.bis.org/

Basel Committee on Banking Supervision – Customer Due Diligence for Banks
(Basel, October 2001)
http://www.bis.org/publ/bcbs85.htm

Basel Committee on Banking Supervision – Prevention of Criminal use of the Banking System for the Purpose of Money Laundering
(Basel, December 1988)
http://www.bis.org/publ/bcbsc137.pdf

United Nations
http://www.un.org/

International Convention for the Suppression of the Financing of Terrorism
(New York, 9 December 1999)

http://untreaty.un.org/English/Terrorism/Conv12.pdf

(Link to current participant list)

http://untreaty.un.org/ENGLISH/Status/Chapter xviii/treaty11.asp

UN Security Council Resolution 1373
(New York, 28 September 2001)

http://daccess-ods.un.org/doc/UNDOC/GEN/N01/557/43/PDF/N0155743.pdf?OpenElement

UN Security Council Resolution 1373 – Counter Terrorism Committee

http://www.un.org/Docs/sc/committees/1373/

UN Convention Against Transnational Organized Crime (Palermo, 12-15 December 2000)

http://www.undcp.org/palermo/convmain.htm

UN Convention Against Illicit Traffic in Narcotic Drugs and Psychotropic Substances
(Vienna, 20 December 1988)

http://www.incb.org/e/conv/1988/index.htm

Transparency International

http://www.wolfsberg-principles.com/index.htm

Global Anti-Money Laundering Guidelines for Private Banking: "The Wolfsberg AML Principles"
(October 2000)

http://www.wolfsberg-principles.com/wolfsberg principles 1st revision.htm

The Suppression of the Financing of Terrorism: "The Wolfsberg Statement"
(Wolfsberg, January 2002)

http://www.wolfsberg-principles.com/wolfsberg principles 1st revision.htm

Financial Action Task Force on Money Laundering (FATF)

FATF - Report on Money Laundering Typologies, 2001-2002

http://www.fatf-gafi.org//pdf/TY2002_en.pdf

FATF - Report on Money Laundering Typologies, 2000-2001

http://www.fatf-gafi.org//pdf/TY2001_cn.pdf

The Financial Crimes Enforcement Network (FinCEN)

SAR Bulletin - Issue 4 "Aspects of Financial Transactions Indicative of Terrorist Funding" (January 2002)

http://www.treas.gov/fincen/sarbul0201-f.pdf

FinCEN Follows the Money: A Local Approach to Identifying and Tracing Criminal Proceeds (January 1999)

http://www.treas.gov/fincen/followme.pdf

Minority Staff of the U.S. Senate Permanent Subcommittee on Investigations - Report on Correspondent Banking: A Gateway for Money Laundering

http://www.senate.gov/~gov_affairs/020501_psi_minority_report.htm

Minority Staff of the U.S. Senate Permanent Subcommittee on Investigations - Private Banking and Money Laundering: A Case Study of Opportunities and Vulnerabilities

http://levin.senate.gov/issues/psireport2.htm

U.S. House Financial Services Subcommittee on Oversight and Investigations Hearing

http://financialservices.house.gov/media/pdf/021202dl.pdf